Meet
Jim Henson

by Louise Gikow

A Bullseye Biography

Random House 🏠 New York

For Rachel and Jamie

MUPPETS, THE MUPPET SHOW, MUPPET BABIES, FRAGGLE ROCK, JIM
HENSON'S MUPPET∗VISION 3D and character names and likenesses are trademarks
of Jim Henson Productions, Inc.

Cover design by Fabia Wargin Design and Creative Media Applications, Inc.
Copyright © 1993 by Jim Henson Productions, Inc.
All rights reserved under International and Pan-American Copyright Conventions.
Published in the United States by Random House, Inc., New York, and simultaneously
in Canada by Random House of Canada Limited, Toronto.

Library of Congress Cataloging-in-Publication Data
Gikow, Louise. Meet Jim Henson / by Louise Gikow.
p. cm.—(A Bullseye biography) SUMMARY: Discusses the life and accomplishments
of the creator of the Muppets, puppet stars of television and the movies.
ISBN 0-679-82691-2
1. Henson, Jim—Juvenile literature. 2. Muppet show (Television program)—
Juvenile literature. 3. Puppeteers—United States—Biography—Juvenile literature.
[1. Henson, Jim. 2. Muppet Show (Television program). 3. Puppeteers.]
I. Title. II. Series. PN1982.H46G55 1993 791.5'3'092—dc20 92-30225

Manufactured in the United States of America 10 9 8 7 6 5 4 3 2 1

Contents

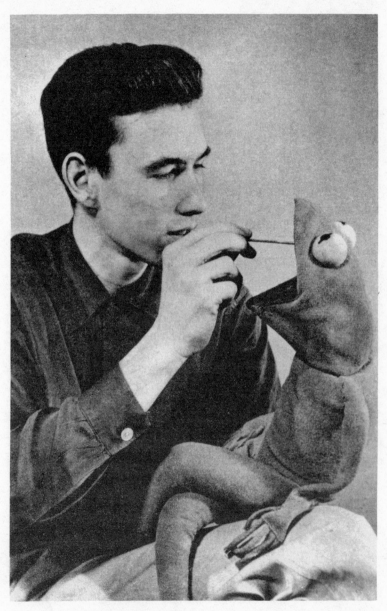

Jim Henson works on the original Kermit.

I

Kermit

It is 1954.

A tall, thin eighteen-year-old kneels in the hallway of his Hyattsville, Maryland, home. He is rummaging through his mother's rag bag. One by one he pulls out pieces of colorful material. He shakes his head. Nothing seems quite right.

Finally the young man finds what he is looking for. It is a large piece of faded green wool—the remains of one of his mother's old coats. The young man smiles a gentle smile. *This*, he thinks, *will probably do just fine.*

Later that week the young man goes to his grandparents' house. They live on the other side of town. The young man's grandfather is sick. Each day different members of the family have been keeping him company.

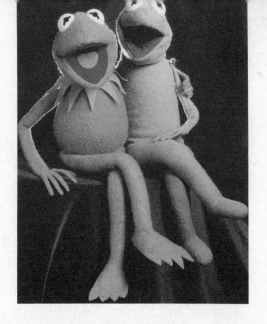

You can always tell the early Kermit from the later Kermit. The early Kermit didn't have a collar. (As you can see, the early Kermit also didn't have flippers! That's because he wasn't a frog yet.)

Today is the young man's turn.

He sits in his grandfather's bedroom and watches the old man lovingly. Then the young man takes out the piece of faded green wool. He takes out a needle. He takes out some thread. Sewing will not disturb his grandfather. But it gives the young man something to do. It helps him pass the time. Besides, he wants to finish the work he has started.

The young man sews slowly and carefully. He can't sew very well. But he manages. He is good with his hands. He likes to draw and to make things. He thinks that someday he might be a cartoonist.

His long slender fingers poke the needle into the soft fabric. He knows what he's after. Bit by bit he carefully coaxes a shape from the cloth.

He puts the cloth shape over his hand. It is a puppet.

The young man moves his thumb and fingers. Every movement shows through the fabric. First the puppet frowns thoughtfully. The young man can almost *see* the puppet think. This creature, whatever it is, is clearly very intelligent.

Then a smile forms at the corners of the

This picture of a "modern" Kermit clearly shows his collar.

puppet's mouth. It is a real and warm smile. The young man smiles back.

Later the young man returns home. He borrows two Ping-Pong balls from his older brother, Paul. He thinks for a while. Then he takes one ball and cuts it in half. He carefully glues each half to the little puppet's face. He draws a circle on each half. Then he draws a line through each circle.

The young man is satisfied. He puts the puppet on again. The Ping-Pong eyes are friendly and wise. The puppet feels comfortable on his hand. In a few days the young man will decide to give the puppet a name.

The name is Kermit.

The young man is Jim Henson.

2
TV

James Maury Henson was born on September 24, 1936, in Greenville, Mississippi. He grew up in nearby Leland, Mississippi.

Jim's father, Paul senior, was an agricultural research biologist. He spent his time studying different plants to see if he could make them grow better and faster. Jim's mother, Betty, was a homemaker. She was devoted to Jim and to Jim's brother, Paul junior, who was two years older than Jim.

When Jim was in fifth grade, his father got a new job that moved the family to Hyattsville, Maryland.

Jim went to school, played, got into trouble, and spent a lot of time with his grandmother Dear. There was no sign that he was any different from his brother, his cousins, or

Jim's mother and father—
Betty and Paul senior.

Jim (left) and his brother, Paul.

Jim's mother, Betty.

Jim as a baby.

any of the other kids in the neighborhood.

But that all changed one day in 1949.

That day thirteen-year-old Jim watched as two deliverymen carried a big cardboard box into his living room. Jim was very excited.

He was finally getting a television set! And in those days, not very many people had TVs in their homes.

The set wasn't just for Jim, of course. His mother, father, and brother would be watching it, too. But Jim was the one who had wanted it. He was the one who had begged his parents until they finally gave in and bought a TV.

Jim's father carefully slit the tape on the top of the box. He opened the flaps. There, glowing and elegant in its wooden cabinet, was the new TV.

Paul senior plugged in the TV and turned it on. A black and white picture flickered to life. It was a small picture. It was only about ten inches across. But Jim was delighted.

"As soon as we got that set, I absolutely loved television," Jim said later. "I loved the idea that what you saw was actually taking place at the same time somewhere else."

Then and there Jim decided that he would work in the television industry one day. And when Jim Henson decided to do something, that was that. He never made a big fuss about anything. He just quietly and steadily worked toward his goals.

To Jim the world was a big, fascinating place. A guy could do almost anything if he had the strength to follow his dreams!

Where did Jim get his self-confidence? Much of it came from his parents. And a lot of it probably came from his mother's mother, Sarah Brown.

Mrs. Brown was known to her family as Dear. And she was very dear to Jim. She was interested in many things, including art. In fact, Dear was a talented painter.

Most of all, though, Dear was interested in Jim and her other grandchildren. When Jim walked through the door of her house, Dear made him feel special. She made him feel as if he were the most important person in the world. She wanted to know everything about what he had done that day. And she always had an encouraging word.

Jim when he was about
two and a half years old.

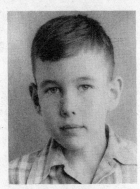

Jim as a
schoolboy.

Jim's grandmother Dear.

Jim (right) poses with his
mother and his brother, Paul.

One day in 1954, when Jim was a senior
in high school, the news he had for Dear was
even more exciting than usual.

Jim had been looking for a job in television since he was sixteen. Until that day,
nobody had wanted to hire him. But some

13

Jim (center) and his family.

Jim, about seventeen years old, in an early studio portrait.

Jim loved cars. He drove to his college graduation in this secondhand Rolls-Royce. He bought it with money he made from puppeteering.

From left to right: Bil Baird, Burr Tilstrom, Jim Henson.

people from WTOP had just visited his high school puppetry club.

WTOP was a local TV station. It broadcast out of Washington, D.C. The station was looking for a puppeteer for a Saturday-morning children's show. But they couldn't afford to pay much. So they had decided to hire a high school student.

This was Jim's chance to work in television!

Jim Henson had watched Burr Tilstrom's puppets on the popular TV show *Kukla, Fran & Ollie*. He had also seen another famous puppeteer, Bil Baird, on television. And Jim had already made a few puppets for the puppetry club.

But Jim had never made a puppet that would appear on TV.

This didn't bother Jim. He went to the library and took out a book about puppets. He studied it from cover to cover. He read about shadow puppets and marionettes and hand puppets. He read about every kind of puppet there was. Then he made three finger puppets. And he and a friend from school took the puppets to WTOP.

They got the job.

3

Studio Days

At first you might not have noticed him.

He stood in the back of the control room at the television studio. He watched the engineers doing their jobs. He was quiet and polite. And he never interrupted. He followed every move and listened to every word.

Jim Henson was beginning his career in television.

Jim loved hanging around the engineers. He would stay after work every Saturday. He would ask them questions about what they did. The engineers liked the quiet, friendly, eager young man.

TV was an exciting business to be in. And the engineers enjoyed sharing what they knew. So they talked, and Jim listened

Jim working on a puppet head. This one was carved out of foam—the same kind of foam that you find in foam mattresses or pillows!

and learned all about television from the ground up.

Television was Jim's first love. In fact, when he first went to work at WTOP, he was much more interested in TV than he was in puppets.

Sure, puppets were fun. But mostly puppets were a way to get Jim a job in TV.

The more Jim worked with puppets, though, the more interested he became in them. Jim liked puppets because he felt that they could show so many more feelings than people could.

Back in the 1950s, when Jim started working in television, human performers had to look a certain way and act a certain way on TV. They couldn't show all their feelings. But a puppet could break through and show many things that human performers couldn't.

For example, maybe the person reading a news report on TV thinks the report is silly. The person may not be able to laugh...but a puppet can.

Puppets can show the real feelings behind the TV masks. They can show happiness, sadness, anger, or just plain silliness. Jim was particularly fond of the silly part.

Jim also enjoyed making puppets. He especially enjoyed making unusual puppets. It was fun to try to build a puppet bird that looked as if it were really flying. It was fun to make a puppet flower that opened its petals and looked alive.

In 1955, just before his nineteenth birthday, Jim entered the University of Maryland. He had decided to study art.

At the same time, Jim was still performing with puppets on television. His first high school job had ended. But WRC-TV, an NBC television station, had hired him to work on another show.

The University of Maryland offered a course in puppeteering. So of course Jim signed up.

Jim was the only freshman in the class. The other students were seniors. Jim was also the only student with any experience.

All art education students had to take puppetry in order to graduate. Well, maybe they had to take it.... But did they have to take it seriously? Most of them didn't think so. They were there to earn the credits they needed for a degree. And they were there to have fun.

Jim soon realized that he probably wasn't going to learn anything new in class. So he decided to do something about it.

Jim started dreaming up the ideas for the puppet shows the class put on. He even wrote one of them and performed many of the puppets. And whenever anyone in the class lost interest, he would talk them into getting involved again.

Jim's enthusiasm fired the other students' interest in puppetry. One of these students was Jane Nebel.

Jane was a young woman from New York. She was interested in ceramics and painting. She was planning to teach after she graduated.

Jane knew almost nothing about puppets. But she liked Jim's boundless energy. And Jim liked the way Jane worked. So when he was hired by WRC-TV to do a new television show, he asked Jane to work with him.

Jane was a senior. She had a decision to make. Should she go into teaching? Or should she work with Jim on the show?

Jane decided on Jim. This decision gave her life a whole new direction. Four years later she and Jim Henson would marry.

Jim's new show, *Sam and Friends*, started him in a whole new direction, too. And a wonderful direction it was. It would lead him to millions of children and adults around the world.

4

Sam and Friends

Jim Henson kneels down behind a five-foot six-inch wall. On his hand is Kermit. Kermit is wearing a blond wig. He sits on the wall.

A record player plays a popular song, "I've Grown Accustomed to Your Face." Rosemary Clooney, the famous entertainer, is singing the song. Kermit is lip-synching.

Also "onstage" is a monster puppet named Yorick. Yorick is performed by Jane Henson. He has a napkin over his head. The napkin has a smiling face on it.

While Kermit sings, Jane makes Yorick grab the napkin with his mouth. Slowly Yorick eats the napkin. Then he notices Kermit. Kermit notices Yorick, too. Yorick makes Kermit very nervous.

Yorick slides over and begins to nibble on

Jim and two of his stars from Sam and Friends: *Yorick and Kermit.*

Kermit's leg. Kermit pulls away. Yorick grabs Kermit's arm. Kermit pulls away again. But Yorick is determined.

Finally he gets a good hold on Kermit's leg. Then he slowly drags Kermit offstage. What will happen to Kermit is anyone's guess.

This funny, weird little skit is a good example of the work Jim did on *Sam and Friends. Sam and Friends* was a five-minute local show. It aired twice a day, at 6:25 P.M. and 11:25 P.M.

Sam and Friends starred a small group of characters. Sam was the only human. The other characters weren't anything at all.

Yorick was a sort of monster. Harry and Moldy Hay and Mushmelon were...well, nobody knew what they were. Kermit wasn't even a frog yet. He was just a green lizardlike critter called Kermit.

But all of the characters had strong personalities. And what made the show funny was how all these different personalities acted together.

Sam and Friends was set up like a small variety show. Characters came out and sang songs or performed in some way.

In the beginning, the characters mostly lip-synched to popular songs. While they were performing, the other characters would appear onstage and do whatever they felt like doing. No one ever knew what was going to happen next. But it was usually funny.

It also could be a surprise. These were the

days before videotape had been invented. This meant that the show was performed live in front of the cameras. What the performers did in the studio was on TV the moment that they did it—mistakes and all!

Luckily Jim had a lot of freedom doing *Sam and Friends*. For one thing, it was a local show. There were only a few nationally broadcast TV shows then. So if Jim did make mistakes, it wasn't as if he was embarrassing himself in front of the entire country.

Besides, it was a good time to be creating interesting new work for TV. In the 1950s the world was open to a slew of new ideas. Jazz music was all the rage. So were new forms of poetry. Artists were painting big, unusual, sloppy canvases. And Jim's funny, strange work was a part of it all.

Having a daily show was a great experience for Jim. He needed a lot of material for the show. That meant he had to constantly come up with new ideas. And working on *Sam and Friends* also taught Jim many more things about puppets and TV.

Jim discovered, for example, that soft puppet faces worked very well on TV. Most puppets before this time had hard, rigid faces. That's because they were meant to be seen only from a distance, on a puppet stage. On TV they looked stiff and fake. But the soft, flexible puppets that Jim and Jane put over their hands seemed almost alive. The puppets' faces could express many more thoughts and emotions than puppet faces ever had before.

Jim also began experimenting with TV cameras. He set them up much closer to the puppets than they had ever been before. This was important for two reasons. First, Jim's

Jim, Jane, and most of the Sam and Friends *cast.*

softer puppet faces looked wonderful in closeups. Second, Jim was able to get rid of the boxlike puppet stage that all other puppeteers were still using.

Instead of using a puppet stage, Jim had the camera "frame" the action. This made Jim's puppets look like regular actors to the home audience. It made them look as if they were moving about in a real place.

Jim also worked out a way for the puppeteers to "see" what they were doing more easily. It was hard for the puppeteers to tell how things looked when they were holding puppets over their heads. So Jim set up television monitors around the floor where he worked. These monitors showed exactly what people would see on their television screens.

Jim and his puppeteers would constantly look down at the monitors. That way they could see how their performances looked as they went along. This made for much better, more realistic puppeteering.

At the same time Jim was making *Sam and Friends* he also began making some unusual commercials for companies like La Choy Food Products and the Ralston Purina Company Limited. The commercials were unusual because they were funny.

Nowadays we see funny ads everywhere. But back then commercials were serious. And they were usually boring! Jim was one of the first people to make funny commercials. After Jim, commercials were never the same again.

Jim's commercials were funny for some of the same reasons that *Sam and Friends* was funny. He had his puppets say—and do—surprising and funny things. He had them say things people wished they could say but were afraid to say on TV.

Today, in a file at Jim Henson Productions headquarters, there is a piece of lined yellow paper. On it, in Jim's handwriting, is a script for a Wilson & Co., Inc., Meats commercial. The commercial starred two puppets called Scoop and Skip. It went:

SCOOP: My favorite food is Wilson's Certified Bacon.
(*Skip appears...*)
SCOOP: Where's my Wilson's Certified Bacon?
SKIP: I ate it.
SCOOP: How did you like it?
SKIP: Delicious.
SCOOP: How do you like *this*?
WHUNK-CRACK-SPLINTER
SKIP: Personally, I prefer the bacon.

No one had ever shown appreciation for Wilson's Certified Bacon—or any product—in quite the same way that Jim did in this script. (The WHUNK-CRACK-SPLINTER stood for the fact that Scoop was hitting poor Skip over the head!) But people loved it. Jim's commercials were so successful that, all told, he made hundreds of them for more than forty companies.

Interestingly, it was Jim's voice that came out of the mouths of both of the puppets in the Wilson's Certified Bacon commercial. Jim was beginning to use his own voice on television more and more. It was a voice that people would learn to love. It was the voice of Kermit, Ernie, and a host of other wonderful characters.

One day in April 1956, Jim's family got some terrible news. Paul Henson, Jim's older brother, had been killed in a car accident in Florida. Paul was only twenty-two years old.

There are no words to describe how much the loss of his gentle, sweet older brother hurt Jim.

The two boys had been very close. Paul had always looked out for Jim, and Jim loved Paul very much. But it is possible that Paul's death may have increased Jim's determination to work hard and make his family proud of him.

In any case, Jim managed to pull himself

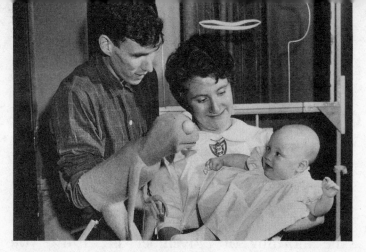

Jim, Jane, baby Lisa (their first child), and friend.
Jim and Jane would have four more children.

together and get on with his life.

One day Jim and Jane were sitting and talking about *Sam and Friends*. Jim probably said something to Jane like, "We need a name for these guys!" So they started to think about it.

It didn't take Jim long to come up with the word "Muppet." It was a nice combination of the words "marionette" and "puppet." Mostly, though, Jim liked the sound of it.

And so the Muppets were born.

5

Sesame Street

If you had been watching public television on the morning of November 11, 1969, you might have heard this song for the first time: "Sunny day, chasing the clouds away. On my way to where the air is sweet. Can you tell me how to get, how to get to Sesame Street?"

Then you would have seen a little girl named Sally walk onto this place called Sesame Street. She had just moved into the neighborhood. A man named Gordon was showing her around.

That day you would have seen Sally meet Gordon's wife, Susan, and his friends Bob and Mr. Hooper. You'd also have seen an eight-foot-two-inch-tall six-year-old bird named Big Bird, a grouch named Oscar, two friends named Bert and Ernie, and a

Jim performing Kermit.

frog named Kermit (yes, he had recently become one!).

One other thing you would have seen on TV that day was Jim Henson himself! Jim made a rare television appearance on that first episode of *Sesame Street*. He was wearing one of the brightly colored striped shirts he loved. And he was juggling three balls. His one line? "Three balls."

Of course, Jim had lots of other lines on

the show, too. He was performing Ernie, Kermit, and a few other Muppet characters as well.

Nowadays it's hard to imagine *Sesame Street* without Muppets. But it could have happened. On the day in 1967 when Joan Ganz Cooney called Jim about working on the new show, he wasn't really sure he should do it.

Joan Ganz Cooney was an Emmy Award–winning producer for Channel 13, the educational TV station in New York. She had recently done a study about children and

Jim and the other puppeteers have to hold their puppets over their heads so that the puppeteers can't be seen. This means everything else has to be high up too, including the cameras and the sets.

television. The study showed that many children were spending more hours a week watching television than they were spending in school!

Joan Cooney had a vision of a new kind of educational television show. It would help teach kids to read and count while they watched TV. She wanted Jim to work on the show.

By now Jim and his Muppets had been making successful commercials for many years. He and Jane were living comfortably in Greenwich, Connecticut, with their four children—Lisa, Cheryl, Brian, and John. (A fifth daughter, Heather, would be born in late 1970.)

Jim's Muppets were also appearing on lots of variety shows. They had been on *The Ed Sullivan Show* and *The Perry Como Show*. And Jim was a regular guest for three years on *The Jimmy Dean Show*, performing Rowlf the Dog. Rowlf was Jim's first regular character on a national TV show.

Things were certainly hopping for Jim Henson. But what should he do about Joan Ganz Cooney and her offer?

Jim was afraid that if he worked with Joan on her new show, people might start thinking his work was just for kids. Jim didn't want people to think that. He wanted his work to continue to be for people of all ages.

Jim had always felt that puppets weren't treated with enough respect in the United States. He had traveled to Europe when he was in college. There he had discovered that people didn't think puppets were only for kids. Puppets there perform for adults as well as children.

Would doing Joan Cooney's show mean that people would think Jim's puppets were "for kids only"?

But then Jim thought about his own four young children. He knew how wonderful a show like this could be for them and for lots of other kids. Plus, Jim had a lot of respect for kids. He liked their honesty and sense of humor. And he thought kids were great audiences.

So Jim decided to work with Joan on the new show.

By this time Jim had been joined by some people who would be very important to the Muppets. These included Jerry Juhl, Don Sahlin, and Frank Oz.

Jerry Juhl had worked with Jim since 1961. He had been hired as a puppeteer to replace Jane, who was busy at the time with

A group of Sesame Street puppeteers with their puppets up. They are, from left to right, Marty Robinson, Jim Henson, and David Rudman.

On Sesame Street *with the original cast from the show. Many of them still work on* Sesame Street *today!*

babies Lisa and Cheryl. But Jerry's true love was writing.

Jim loved writing with Jerry. Day after summer day Jim and Jerry would spend time in Jim's backyard. They would each take turns lying in the hammock. There they would come up with lots of ideas for skits and screenplays. Later Jerry would become the head writer on *The Muppet Show*. He would also become the writer of many of Jim's other projects.

Don Sahlin was a talented puppet builder. He had worked with Burr Tilstrom. He built Rowlf and would design many more characters for Jim. Don was the person who perfected the "look" of the Muppets, especially the *Sesame Street* Muppets.

Frank Oz was a young and brilliant puppeteer when he joined Jim in August 1963. That was right after Frank had graduated

Don Sahlin built many of the early Muppets, including the Sesame Street *Muppets. Here, Jim and Don work on Bert.*

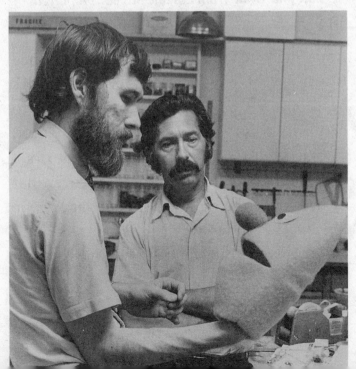

Bert and Ernie from Sesame Street. *Jim played Ernie, and Frank Oz played Bert.*

from high school. At first, he performed Rowlf's right paw. (Jim performed Rowlf's head and left paw.) Frank later went on to perform Miss Piggy, Fozzie Bear, Bert, Cookie Monster, and Grover, among others.

It didn't take long for Jim to discover that he had made the right decision about *Sesame Street*. The show was an instant hit, and the *Sesame Street* Muppets became beloved friends of children all over the country.

Versions of *Sesame Street* have since played all around the world. Jim Henson's Muppets have become famous in such countries as Great Britain, France, Germany, Mexico, Israel, and Kuwait.

Working on a valued and award-winning show for children was a terrific experience for Jim. But he still hadn't given up his dream of puppet shows for kids *and* grown-ups. He had already created a number of Muppet television specials that were for family audiences. These included *Hey Cinderella!* and *The Frog Prince*.

But Jim also wanted to create a weekly evening series that the whole family would watch. And he was sure he could do it with the Muppets.

6

The Muppet Show

Seven men and women are standing behind a model of a Viking ship. The ship is about eight feet long. It is up on stilts. Seven pairs of legs can be seen below it. One pair belongs to Jim Henson.

The men and women hold pig puppets high above their heads. The pigs are dressed in Viking costumes. To the audience it looks as if the pigs are on the ship.

Below the ship, TV monitors are everywhere. The monitors show the puppeteers what the scene will look like on television.

The pigs in the ship are singing "In the Navy." It's a silly song for pigs to be singing. (In fact, the whole *idea* of Viking pigs is pretty silly.)

The Muppet Show is in production.

The cast of The Muppet Show. *Five of the characters shown were performed by Jim. They are Kermit, Rowlf, Dr. Teeth, Waldorf, and Link Hogthrob.*

Jim Henson had always wanted to do a half-hour Muppet variety show. He had wanted to do this even in the days before *Sesame Street*. Jim's idea for the show was this: It would be about the Muppets trying to put on their *own* variety show.

The show would feature the Muppets plus a different famous guest star each week. During his Muppet appearances on such TV shows as *The Jimmy Dean Show*, *The Steve Allen Show*, and even *Sesame Street*, Jim had discovered that actors and actresses loved working with Muppets. And the Muppets worked very well with people, too.

Most important, since these were Muppets, they would get into lots of trouble while

Steve Martin with Kermit on The Muppet Show. *The man beneath the frog is, of course, Jim.*

putting on their show. And this trouble would be very funny.

All the things that Jim had learned about comedy would be used in the show. One of the main things he had learned was that words were not as important as actions. In the world of puppetry, visual gags were the most important of all. Things had to *happen* to the puppets...and the funnier the better.

"It's important to understand," Jim once said, "that these puppets are not just characters up there telling jokes. If they just stand there...the whole thing will fall flat. The humor only holds if there's visual interaction between the characters."

This means it isn't funny to see Fozzie Bear *telling* a joke. What's funny is if something *happens* to Fozzie while he's telling the joke. For example, it's funny if Fozzie can't say the punchline because he's just been hit in the face with a cream pie or has slipped on a banana peel.

That's why, when you see a performance

by a Muppet, he or she will usually be *doing* something funny—not just talking about it.

Jim had the show all figured out. He *knew* it would be a success. But the American networks weren't sure. Puppets on prime time? they all wondered. Would grownups really want to watch puppets on prime time TV?

Jim knew they would. But the network executives were dragging their feet. That's when something amazing happened. Sir Lew Grade, a well-known English entertainment producer, stepped in. Hardly anyone in England had even heard of Jim Henson. But Sir Lew Grade wanted to do the show...*if* Jim would do it in England.

No problem! In 1976, Jim packed up the puppeteers, puppet builders, and writers. They headed for the studio in England. There Jim worked six days a week for months at a time to produce *The Muppet Show.*

The Muppet Show wasn't easy to make. In fact, working with Muppets is much harder than working with actors.

The Muppet Show *in production. Puppeteers, from left to right: Dave Goelz, Jerry Nelson, Jim Henson, Frank Oz, Richard Hunt.*

For one thing, getting a Muppet to follow a simple stage direction like PICK UP THE BALL isn't easy. It's not that Muppets aren't cooperative. It's just that many of them simply can't pick up a ball. That's because they are hand-and-rod puppets. Their hands are just flat pieces of fabric. Anything they hold has to be taped to their hands while the audience isn't looking.

To operate a hand-and-rod puppet a puppeteer puts one hand inside the puppet's head. In his or her other hand the puppeteer holds two rods. These are almost invisible on-camera. They are connected to the puppet's hands. They allow the puppeteer to move the puppet's arms and hands (*see photo*, page 33).

It takes a lot of skill and practice to bring a Muppet to life. Multiply one Muppet times the thirty or so that were featured on an average half-hour show. (This includes Piggy, Gonzo, Fozzie, Statler and Waldorf, Scooter, the band, the other principals, and the talking animals, vegetables, and minerals.) Then you can begin to understand just how complicated it was to produce *The Muppet Show*!

But all the hard work paid off. *The Muppet Show* became one of the most popular television shows ever. At the height of its popularity more than 235 *million* people were watching Kermit and company every week.

The Muppet Show won many international television awards and ran for five years. From Spain to Senegal, from the United Kingdom to the the United States, it

Miss Piggy— performed by Frank Oz—rose from the chorus line of The Muppet Show *to become one of its biggest stars.*

was a hit with adults and children alike.

For *The Muppet Show*, Jim, Frank Oz, Jerry Juhl, and art director Michael K. Frith had invented a partner for Kermit. This partner was a comedian who was afraid he wasn't funny. His name was Fozzie Bear.

Fozzie Bear became a popular character on the show. But he wasn't the only character to work closely with Kermit. During the first year of production, a pig from the chorus started to force herself into the spotlight. She was performed by Frank Oz. She was chubby, funny, and...well...pushy.

As the year went by, the pig started to wear nicer clothes. She even began to *look* better. The shape of her nose changed. Her eyes got bigger. And she got even...well... pushier.

By the second season, Miss Piggy had almost taken over the show. She was to become one of the funniest and most glamorous characters of her time. A pig had come out of the chorus...and become a star!

7

Movies

Jerry Juhl once said that if *The Muppet Show* were a basketball game, the score would always be Chaos 98, Frog 99.

That certainly seemed to be true. Lots of things were always going on around Kermit. But somehow he was always able to solve any problems that might come up.

In this way, Kermit was a lot like Jim Henson. Jim always had lots of things going on around him at the same time, too. But he was always calm and in control.

Jim had always been interested in movies. The first film he had ever seen was *The Wizard of Oz*. He later said that it was probably still his favorite movie.

There was only one thing he hadn't liked about it. That was the MGM lion that

Kermit stands up to Doc Hopper in The Muppet Movie. *Doc Hopper owns a chain of restaurants that specialize in...gulp...frogs' legs!*

roared at the beginning of every movie produced by MGM Studios. "My parents told me that when the MGM lion came on, it really scared me," Jim said. "For a long time the thing I remembered best about the movie was the lion."

Jim's interest in the movies continued when he got older. While he was making commercials, he bought a motion picture camera. He used it to take moving pictures of paintings he was doing. He'd paint a stroke, then film it. Then he'd paint another and film it, and so on. Then he'd watch as the paintings "came to life" on film.

Throughout the 1960s, Jim made a number of short films. One of them, *Timepiece*, was nominated for an Academy Award.

While he was working on *The Muppet Show*, Jim also made a series of feature-length movies starring the Muppets. They were *The Muppet Movie* (1979), *The Great Muppet Caper* (1981), and *The Muppets Take Manhattan* (1984).

But *The Muppet Show* and the Muppet movies weren't the only things keeping Jim busy. In 1976, Jim created some puppets for the hit comedy show *Saturday Night Live*.

These characters were on the show for only one season. Few people remember them. But Jim really liked them. They were different from the Muppets. They looked more like living creatures...even though they were pretty strange. They didn't look like creatures you would ever see on Earth!

The *Saturday Night Live* puppets looked more alive partly because they had taxidermists' eyes. These are the eyes used in animals that are stuffed for museum displays.

Jim also continued to produce more television specials. One of these was *Emmet Otter's Jug-Band Christmas* (1978). *Emmet Otter* starred another new group of characters. They were more realistic puppets than the pigs and bears of *The Muppet Show*. But they were just as lovable.

These new kinds of animals and creatures got Jim interested in making new kinds of puppets. They would be much more complicated than the original Muppets. They would have eyes that squinted, eyelids that blinked, and foreheads that wrinkled. They would be made of material that looked more like real skin or fur. And it would take more than one puppeteer to operate them.

"I could see that it would take an awful lot of technical know-how to make it work,"

Jim sitting on the miniature set of Emmet Otter's
Jug-Band Christmas.

Jim later said. "But we had the beginning of
a team of people who could tackle that. We
could never have tried something like *The
Dark Crystal* even a few years earlier,
because until recently we did not have the
performers, the puppet builders, or the tech-
nicians who could handle the problems
involved."

The Dark Crystal, made in 1981–82, was
Jim's first fantasy film with puppets—but
without the Muppets. It was the story of a
world where good, gentle creatures called
Mystics and evil creatures called Skeksis
lived. The world was no longer in balance. It

was now ruled by the Skeksis alone. It became the job of a young boy and girl, themselves members of another race, to put everything right again.

Jim made a second fantasy film called *Labyrinth* in 1986. *Labyrinth* was the story of a girl whose baby brother is kidnapped by the king of the goblins. The goblin king was played by rock star David Bowie.

Both films used Jim's new, complicated puppets. The character Hoggle in *Labyrinth*, for example, had one small performer inside of him. Three additional puppeteers were outside. They operated his mouth, blinks, and other facial movements by radio control.

One of these three puppeteers also created

Jen (left) and Kira from The Dark Crystal. *Jen was performed by Jim, and Kira was performed by Kathy Mullen.*

Someone from the shop works on Hoggle, one of the lead characters in Labyrinth.

Hoggle's voice and personality. He was Jim's son Brian, who was a talented performer in his own right.

Most people praised the puppetry in both films. But there were people who didn't like or understand *The Dark Crystal* and *Labyrinth*. Maybe that was because everyone expected Jim's work to be funny and happy. And these movies were darker and more complicated.

But Jim had never wanted to play it safe. He liked taking creative risks. If people didn't like one thing...well, then it was on to another!

8

A Special View of the World

Imagine a glowing underground world full of tunnels and canyons and pools. Now picture a race of beings who are eighteen inches tall. They come in all sorts of bright colors. And they love to laugh, sing, and play. They only have to work twenty minutes a week. And they love radishes more than any other food!

What have you got? Fraggles! And where do they live? Fraggle Rock!

In 1983 audiences saw Jim Henson's new show, *Fraggle Rock*, on TV for the first time. The Fraggles shared their underground world with two other groups. There were the Doozers, little six-inch green characters who loved to work. And then there were the Gorgs, three giants who lived above Fraggle Rock.

Jim with the Fraggles of Fraggle Rock.

The Gorgs didn't like the Fraggles very much. Junior Gorg had a particular problem with Fraggles. They were always eating the beautiful radishes he grew in his garden!

The Fraggles, the Doozers, and the Gorgs were very different from one another. They didn't understand each other at all. That's why none of them got along very well. But all of them needed one another to live—even though they didn't know it. So they had to learn to live together. *Fraggle Rock* was Jim's own quiet way of speaking out for peace and understanding in the world.

Jim Henson used many different kinds of puppets in *Fraggle Rock*. The Fraggles were regular hand-and-rod puppets. The Doozers were almost entirely radio controlled. They were a bit like tiny robots. The Gorgs were giant puppets, almost seven feet tall.

One performer operated the Gorg's eyes and mouth through radio control. A second performer was inside each Gorg. This performer actually used a tiny video monitor *inside the puppet* in order to see where he or she was going! The camera for the monitor was inside the Gorg's head. It looked out through the eyes. The people who invented this system jokingly called it Gorgvision.

Fraggle Rock wasn't the only work through which Jim Henson showed his concern for our planet and the people and animals that live on it. Jim made many public

Kermit and Fozzie in a public-service announcement about recycling. In it, the Muppets use the old joke "What's snoo? I don't know. What's snoo with you?"

service announcements, too. A public service announcement is a small advertisement that TV stations run for free. In these, Jim used Kermit and the other Muppets to spread the good word about peace, good fellowship, and respect for our environment.

As usual, Jim was ahead of his time. But he had always felt that there was nothing you couldn't do if you put your mind to it. That included saving the world. He really believed that he and his Muppets could make a difference in people's lives. And they did.

9

Muppet Babies

In the movie *The Muppets Take Manhattan* there's a very special scene. Piggy imagines that she and Kermit have grown up together in a nursery. For these five minutes of film, Jim and his creative director, Michael K. Frith, developed a group of adorable baby Muppets.

In the movie the babies sing a song and play nursery games. Little Rowlf pounds on his toy piano. Kermit rides a hobbyhorse. Fozzie and Gonzo drive a fire truck. Piggy swings on a swing.

In 1984 the baby Muppets appeared in movie theaters all over the country. Audiences couldn't help smiling. Little Kermit and Piggy and Fozzie and Gonzo and Scooter and Rowlf were adorable!

The original Muppet Babies, who first appeared in
The Muppets Take Manhattan.

When the people who ran CBS-TV saw the baby Muppets, they smiled, too. They decided the babies should star in their own Saturday-morning cartoon show.

At first Jim wasn't sure this was a good idea. He had never done an animated show before. Plus, he didn't really like most Saturday-morning cartoons. But he decided that he would do it if he could create something he felt was worthwhile.

What would be worthwhile to say to kids watching Saturday-morning TV? Something

Jim examines an original cel of Baby Piggy, created for the Muppet Babies' animated TV show. Cels are paintings on clear plastic that are used for animation.

about how wonderful it is to use your imagination, Jim thought.

The Muppet Babies usually stay close to home, just like children everywhere. But they also travel all over the world and through time. They do this through the power of their imaginations. Books, music, toys—all of these things and more lead the Muppet Babies to imagine wild and wonderful adventures.

In addition to the first six babies, Jim

added Baby Animal and Baby Skeeter to the family. (Skeeter was Scooter's twin sister.) He also added a nanny, who is seen only from the waist down—the way small children see grownups!

Children loved the Muppet Babies. The show ran for many years. It also won five Emmy Awards. Jim had achieved his goal. He and his company had created something very worthwhile for Saturday-morning TV. They had created something he could be proud of.

10

A Great Loss

It looked as if Jim Henson's Muppets would last forever. Kermit and the gang were known and loved by people all over the world.

But in the late 1980s Jim realized that he had lots of other things he wanted to do. He saw that he was going to have less and less time for the original Muppets. And he wanted the characters to last as long as possible. That's why he contacted The Walt Disney Company.

Disney seemed to be the perfect place for the Muppets. Hadn't Mickey Mouse been going strong for more than sixty years? And Jim loved the Disney theme parks. The Muppets would feel right at home there.

May 1990 was to be an exciting month

for Jim. The deal with Disney had not yet been finalized. But Jim was already working on some Disney projects. He was just finishing a 3-D Muppet movie for the Disney theme parks. It was to be an inspired example of technical achievement and classic Muppet humor. And he was already planning new TV specials and feature films.

Jim was working nonstop. He was flying constantly between his new headquarters in Los Angeles and his other offices in New York and England. He was also busy taping a new season of *Sesame Street*, performing Kermit, Ernie, and his other characters.

One day Jim came down with what he thought was a cold. A few days later, on a Friday, he flew to North Carolina to visit his father. When he returned to New York that Sunday, the cold had gotten worse. He thought it was just the flu.

On Monday, Jim canceled his appointments. That's when everyone knew how sick he was feeling. Jim *never* canceled appointments. On Tuesday he went into the hospital. It turned out that he didn't have a regular flu. He had a rare form of streptococcus infection.

Phone calls were made from the hospital and from Jim's office. His family and friends were alerted. One by one, those who could reach the hospital did. They came to be with Jim. They came to give him strength.

Everyone was shocked that Jim's life could really be in danger. He was hardly ever sick. He was only fifty-three years old. And he had so much more to do.

The doctors worked hard to stop the infection. But the illness was too strong.

Early Wednesday morning, on May 16, 1990, Jim Henson died.

Five days later, more than five thousand people crowded the Cathedral of St. John the Divine in New York City. They were there for Jim's memorial service. (In July another beautiful service was held in St. Paul's Cathedral in London.)

St. John the Divine was packed. Many people had to be turned away at the door. Some waited outside, just to be close. They shivered with cold. Though it was spring, the weather was chilly and gray.

Inside the cathedral, many people wore bright colors. The colors were Jim's own idea. Four years before, he had carefully written some notes about what he'd like to have happen at his memorial service. He just didn't know that it would take place so soon.

Muppet butterflies had been placed on many of the seats in the cathedral. Each was brightly colored. Each was connected to a two-foot wire. Puppet builders in the Muppet workshop had stayed up all night making them. Men, women, and children filed into the seats. They picked up the butterflies and held them in their laps. No one was exactly sure what to do with them.

A Dixieland band marched slowly up the aisle through a garden of flowers and family

Fellow performers and Muppets sing a song at Jim's memorial service.

pictures. (The band had been Jim's idea, too.) Then the service began.

People who knew Jim spoke about him. Each person told a silly or funny or touching story about the Jim they loved. Frank Oz spoke of working with Jim late into the night. He recalled how wonderful it was to watch Jim laugh until he cried.

Big Bird walked to the front of the cathedral. In a small, sad voice he sang, "Bein' Green" for his friend Jim.

Later Cheryl Henson read some of Jim's writings. One thing Jim wrote was this: "When I was young, my ambition was to be one of the people who makes a difference in this world. My hope still is to leave this world a little bit better than it was when I got here."

Then Brian Henson read from a letter Jim left for his five children. "Please watch out for each other and love and forgive everybody," it said. "It's a good life, enjoy it."

At one point during the service, Kermit's voice came on over the loudspeakers. Kermit was singing "The Rainbow Connection." Slowly, one by one, people began to sing. They picked up the familiar refrain.

And slowly, one by one, the butterflies began to soar and dip. They swooped and darted in time to the music. "Someday we'll find it, the rainbow connection, the lovers, the dreamers, and me." The great cathedral was filled with a sea of fluttering Muppet butterflies.

The voices of Jim's friends and admirers blended with Kermit's voice. To everyone in the cathedral it was the voice of a special friend—the voice of Jim Henson.

11

The Future

It is late in December 1992.

Kids and grownups file into the full-size reproduction of the Muppet Theater at the Disney/MGM Studios Theme Park at Walt Disney World. (Even though the Disney-Muppet merger did not go through, the two companies still work together on many projects.)

Everyone puts on a pair of 3-D glasses. The room darkens—and before everyone's delighted eyes, Kermit appears. He looks as if he were right there in the theater with the audience. He tells them about the wonderful movie they are about to see. It is called *Jim Henson Presents Muppet*Vision 3D*. It is full of terrific 3-D effects.

"It'll be a swell demonstration," Kermit

Kermit and Fozzie in an advertisement for Jim
Henson Presents Muppet∗Vision 3D.

promises. "We won't show you any cheap
3-D tricks."

Fozzie Bear pops out of the screen. "Did
you say cheap 3-D tricks?" he asks. Then he
performs every cheap 3-D trick in the book.
He opens a can—and snakes fly out from the
screen. A trick flower sprays water on the
audience. Kermit is upset. The audience is
delighted.

Thousands of miles away, in a living
room in Chicago, Illinois, a three-year-old

73

girl sits in front of a TV set with her mom. She is watching Ernie on *Sesame Street*. He is singing a song about living on the moon.

Ernie looks wistfully out his Sesame Street window into the night. Then he decides he'd much rather be living here on Earth with all his friends.

The little girl turns to her mother. "More Ernie," she says.

The same day, in a television studio in Los Angeles, a popular show called *Dinosaurs* is being videotaped. It stars a whole new family of dinosaur and other puppets. Brian Henson

In February 1991, some school-children made this Valentine's Day banner in Jim's honor.

Kermit and company star in The Muppet Christmas Carol.

stands nearby. He is making sure that everything goes well.

And in December 1992, in a movie theater in London, England, Kermit and Piggy are singing a song. They are starring in a movie called *The Muppet Christmas Carol*. It

Jim with his most well known creation—
Kermit the Frog.

is the first movie to star the Muppets since
1984. It also stars Michael Caine as Scrooge.
And it has been directed by Brian Henson—
the new head of Jim's company.

Jim Henson's spirit lives on. It lives in the
work of his company. His family and friends

are inspired by Jim's vision. They continue to create new characters and stories.

And Jim's spirit lives in Kermit and Ernie. It lives in Guy Smiley and the Swedish Chef, in Rowlf, Dr. Teeth, Cantus the Minstrel from *Fraggle Rock*, and in all of Jim's other wonderful characters. We can see them whenever we want. All we have to do is turn on the TV or watch a videotape—and Jim is with us again.

LOUISE GIKOW has worked for Jim Henson Productions since 1984, and during that time has written many children's songs and more than fifty children's books. She often worked with Jim and misses him very much.

Bullseye Biographies

Meet Jim Henson

Meet John F. Kennedy